For I am reckoning that the sufferings of the current era do not deserve the glory about to be revealed for us. (Romans 8:18)

You Think *You* Have it Tough?

Dr. Tom Taylor

You Think YOU Have it Tough?
Copyright © 2018-2025, Dr. Tom Taylor
All rights reserved.

No part of this book may be reproduced without written permission from the publisher, except by a reviewer who may quote brief passages in a review; nor may any part of this book be reproduced, stored in a retrieval system or transmitted in any form without written permission from the publisher.

Manufactured in the United States of America

Published by

www.WholeLifeWholeHealth.com

ISBN: 978-1-929921-08-9 (Paperback)
978-1-929921-09-6 (E-Pub)

Unless otherwise noted, Scriptures are quoted from the Concordant Literal New Testament ©1983, and the Concordant Version of the Old Testament ©2012, by the Concordant Publishing Concern, and are used with its kind permission. (www.Concordant.org)

You Think
You
Have it Tough?

Dedications

To the Father of us all:

I'm constantly amazed at Your patience, but more than that, I'm grateful for it and for Your love, structure and constancy. Forgive me for whining and complaining when things haven't gone my way, or the way I think they should have, as if I knew better or could run things better than You. Sheesh! What an arrogant child I have been!

To my elder Brother, Yeshua:

When I slip and fall, You pick me up without losing a single step on the way to accomplishing the Father's **"purpose of the eons"** (Ephesians 3:11). When I cry out to You, even when I have ignored You until I was desperate and came to the end of myself, You were right there to comfort my heart. The fact is, You're *always* there. I may leave *You*, but You never leave *me*, bless Your heart!

To my wife, Barbara:

How the Father trusted me with His favorite daughter is beyond my comprehension and drops me to my knees in gratitude. You have been a light of love, grace, and selfless service, the likes of which I have never seen before. I am unspeakably grateful for your love, patience, and persistence. If I drew my last breath today, I would die having known the ineffable joy of receiving and giving true love.

Table of Contents

	Introduction	1
1.	What's His Name?	3
2.	The Lord Makes a "House Call"	9
3.	Meet the Mediator	13
4.	"Hosanna!"	17
5.	Bread, Wine, and Water	23
6.	Watch and Pray	33
7.	Silent Witness	39
8.	"Crucify!"	45
9.	"Skull's Place"	55
10.	Another Garden	61
11.	The Lesson	65
12.	Arise!	77
13.	No More Whining!	89
14.	Believe It or Not	97
15.	Is There More?	103
	"Light Up the Scriptures"	105
	"MorningMagicals"	106
	Whole Life Whole Health	107
	References	108
	Online Sources	109
	About the Author	110
	Other Books and E-Books	111
	Endnotes	113

Introduction

Coming to the end of yourself feels like hell, but only when the clutter that usually runs through your mind has gone silent can the Lord finally get a word in edgewise.

The story you're about to read is true; that is, it actually happened, just like the visions of Isaiah, Ezekiel, Daniel, or the Apostle John. They were transported to a realm beyond normal consciousness, yet they were fully conscious. What they saw were events in the future – prophecies – or messages from the Father.

As you'll discover, I didn't see future events, but ones already past, to impart a lesson that changed my life. I pray it changes yours too.

Blessings and joy in your journey,

Dr. Tom Taylor

1

What's His Name?

For You have magnified Your name, Your promise, over all else. (Psalm 138:2b)

In that half-conscious state between sleeping and waking, I heard the Father's voice: *"I've let this go long enough. Restore My Son's Name."* Whether His voice is gentle or firm, affectionate or stern, there's no mistaking the Father's subject, meaning, or direction.

If *your* son's name were, say, *Benjamin*, you might not like hearing people call him *Jack*, and he probably wouldn't appreciate it either. We consider it common courtesy to use a person's correct name. Even if Benjamin lived in another country, his name might sound different, but people would make every effort to pronounce it correctly. We consider it impolite and even disrespectful to change someone's name arbitrarily; yet, that is exactly what the men who translated the Scriptures did to **"the name that is above every name"** (Philippians 2:9).

The name, *Yeshua,* is supposedly a Greek version of the Hebrew name, *Joshua* or *Jehoshua* (Thayer). The *Concordant Literal* version's *Keyword Concordance* disagrees, however. "Jesus" – "ee-eh-sous" in Greek – has *no* particular meaning, and is little more than a "sound-alike" of His proper Hebrew name, "*Yeshua*" (some authorities spell His name, *Yohoshua* or *Yahushua,* but more agree on *Yeshua* than any other).

Hebrew names carry important meanings. *Yeshua* means, literally, "*Yah saves,*" or, as Thayer and Gesenius state, "*Jehovah is salvation.*" Yeshua's family, and His Hebrew brethren, including His apostles, most certainly spoke and wrote His name properly; even Pontius Pilate and the religious authorities clamoring for His crucifixion knew His name. If the Greek translators had been true stewards, they would have rendered it something like, "*Theos-sozo*" ("*God saves*") or "*Kyrios-sozo*" ("*Lord saves*").

The point is that Yeshua's name was unnecessarily altered when the New Testament writings were compiled and translated. Changing the Hebrew *Yeshua* to the Greek *Jesus* has obscured His name's meaning and undermined its power. The significance of Yeshua's name and the importance of using it properly should be obvious, given His commission from the Father to be the Savior of the world.

> *This truly is the Saviour of the world, the Christ.*
> (John 4:42)
>
> *And we have gazed upon Him, and are testifying that the Father has dispatched the Son, the Saviour of the world.* (1 John 4:14)

Why should Yeshua have been called *any* name other than the one His Father gave Him? It seems absurd to have to consider the question, let alone answer it, because the Father was abundantly clear about His Son's name:

> *Now she shall be bringing forth a Son, and you shall be calling His name [Yeshua], for He shall be saving His people from their sins.* (Matthew 1:21)
>
> *And the messenger said to her, "Fear not, Miriam, for you found favor with God. And lo! You shall be conceiving and be pregnant and be bringing forth a Son, and you shall be calling His name [Yeshua]."*
> (Luke 1:30-31)

We quickly discover how serious a matter Yeshua's name is when we grasp the power it conveys:

> *He who is believing in Him is not being judged; yet he who is not believing has been judged already, for he has not believed in the name of the only-begotten Son of God.* (John 3:18)

The Apostle Peter knew Whose name had the power to heal a lame man:

> **Yet Peter said, "Silver and gold I do not possess; yet what I have, this I am giving to you. In the name of Christ Jesus, the Nazarene, walk!"**
>
> **"In the faith of His name, His name gives stability to this man whom you are beholding, with whom, also, you are acquainted, and the faith which is through Him, gives him this unimpaired soundness in front of you all."** (Acts 3:6, 16)

Let's also address Yeshua's title, *"HaMashiach,"* which means *"the Messiah,"* or *"the anointed"* in Hebrew (two other transliterations are *"Mashiyach"* and *"Moshiach"*). We are most familiar with the word, *"Christ,"* from the Greek word, *Christos*, which also means *anointed*. The *Complete Jewish Bible (CJB)* and the *Jewish Orthodox Bible (JOB)* render Hebrew names as their English transliterations, such as *"Yeshua HaMashiach."*

The name, *Jesus*, and His title, *Christ*, appear in this book only in direct quotations; otherwise, you will see His proper Hebrew name, *Yeshua or [Yeshua]*, and title (in English), *the Messiah*.

When you and I call on the Lord by His correct name, perhaps we will discover what Peter declared 2,000 years ago: **"the faith of His name, His name gives stability...and** *the faith which is through Him, gives...unimpaired soundness"* (Acts 3:16).

His name is *Yeshua*. He is *the Messiah*.

Wherefore, also, God highly exalts Him, and graces Him with the name that is above every name, that in the name of [Yeshua] every knee should be bowing, celestial and terrestrial and subterranean, and every tongue should be acclaiming that Christ Jesus is Lord, for the glory of God, the Father.

(Philippians 2:9-11)

Probing Questions:

- Why do you think Yeshua's name was changed into a "sound-alike" Greek word?
- What happens when you try using His correct name?
- Do you know the Father's real name in Hebrew? (You'll find this explained in the book, *Rescuing God From the Ruble of Religion*)
- What differences could it make in your life to know the Father and the Son by their real names?

My Notes:

2

The Lord Makes a "House Call"

Call to Me, and I shall answer you,
And I shall tell you of great things,
And of unsearchable things
   which you have not known. (Jeremiah 33:3)

"Come with me," Yeshua said. I felt like I was standing face to face with Him, even though I was lying on my back in bed on a late spring night. His expression was neither stern nor gentle, but matter-of-fact and clearly all business; this was not a social visit. I realized later that I had experienced a vision, but at the time, it was as real as the page you're reading.

The Father had heard my complaining for several months and I felt close to a breakdown. Nothing was working out the way I had envisioned when I pulled out of northeast Kansas on a warm, bright summer morning, after more than 23 years, bound for New England and a new career as a wellness doctor.

I was on a mission to, *"Take the hell out of health care."* I knew I had *"the gift,"* because the Father Himself had inspired the change five years earlier, from a two-decade-long career in printing and publishing to a profession in a field I knew nothing about when I started. I distinctly remember feeling as if the Father were grabbing me by the collar and saying, *"This is your next thing."* I had just sat up after my first experience with a doctor who specialized in *"bio-energetics,"* a term I'd never heard before that day. It seemed like all the doctor had done was touch a few points on my head and wiggle my feet; all I knew was that I was different when he was finished. I desperately wanted to learn everything I could as quickly as possible, so I could do the same thing, preferably tomorrow! I asked the doctor, *"What do I have to do to learn this?"*

Within a year, I resigned my position in a multi-national corporation and was back in school. At 40 years old, with a mortgage and two teenagers, I stepped out of the illusion of safety and relative comfort into a new world that was exciting, entirely unfamiliar, and sometimes altogether terrifying. I had risked the known for the unknown in every way.

Five years later, barely a year into my new profession, I was frustrated, disillusioned, and disappointed in myself, my efforts to succeed, and even the path I had chosen. My life looked like a backwoods road during a hurricane, made nearly impassible by fallen trees and downed power lines. I felt like I had made the biggest mistake ever, embarking on a new career in a new land; except that I *knew* the Father had guided me through the last five years. Why, then, did everything appear to be such a miserable failure?

I didn't know whether the Lord showed up that night – just in time, too – out of sympathy for my pain, or because I was making such a racket. I soon learned that He had come in His office as the **"mediator of God and mankind"** (1 Timothy 2:5). I had a "beef" with the Father, and Yeshua came to, *"intervene, either in order to make or to restore peace and friendship."*[1] He taught me by His own example one of the most important lessons I've ever learned.

> **A broken and crushed heart, O Elohim,**
> **You shall not despise.** (Psalm 51:17b)

Probing Questions:

- How do we know the Father is leading us?
- Why does the Father seem to wait until we can hardly take it anymore before He sends help?

My Notes:
_____
_____
_____
_____
_____
_____
_____
_____
_____
_____
_____

3

Meet the Mediator

For there is one God, and one Mediator of God and mankind, a Man, Christ Jesus. (1 Timothy 2:5)

Yeshua took me into a richly paneled boardroom. The carpeting was plush and the incandescent lighting cast a soft glow from a source I could not see. Three dark brown leather executive chairs were placed around a large, highly polished, round-cornered, rectangular conference table.

The Father sat at the head of the table to my left. I couldn't make Him out exactly, but I knew it was Him. He sat silent as Yeshua motioned for me to take the seat nearest me. Yeshua sat down directly across from me and said, *"I understand you're unhappy. Your life seems hard and you feel alone, even abandoned by the Father. I know how you feel; I've been there too."*

I suppose I should have already known, but suddenly, I realized that both He and the Father had been listening to me and watching me all along. Later, I came to realize that they not only observe our lives, but that every detail about them is progressing along a path leading toward the Father, which He mapped out before the eons themselves began.

> **And my days, all of them were written upon Your scroll;**
> **The days, they were formed when there was not one of them.** (Psalm 139:16)

Yeshua held out His hands, resting them on the table, palms up. I saw the scars where the nails had been driven into His flesh.

"*Has anyone done this to you yet?*" He asked, pointing to His wrists. There was, of course, no answer needed to His question, and without waiting for one, He said, "*We have heard your complaints and I came to mediate your dispute.*"

The Father remained silent and never moved. Yeshua continued, "*The Father asks you to be conciliated to Him, forgiving Him for what His love and purpose for you has required.*"

My mind raced. The Father is asking *me* to forgive *Him*? He's not angry with me about whining over my circumstances and even cursing Him? You're telling me that the Father planned all this before time began, so He *knows* – in fact, He knew long ago – how this looks and feels to me? So, You, Brother Yeshua, aren't here pleading *my* case to the *Father*, but you're actually pleading *His* case to *me*?

I didn't have to voice my thoughts, because I knew that they were exposed to the Father and to Yeshua as if I were speaking them aloud. Neither of them answered my questions verbally, and I knew that the questions themselves contained the answers, as if the Lord were saying, *"Yes, that's exactly what I'm saying."*

Finally, Yeshua said, *"I want to show you something."*

> O Yahweh, You have investigated me and are knowing me;
> You Yourself know my sitting down and my rising up;
> You understand my thought from afar;
> My path and my pallet You have measured off,
> And for all my ways You have made provision.
> For though there be no declaration on my tongue,
> Behold, O Yahweh, You know it all.
> Back and front, You have besieged me,
> And You set Your palm upon me.
> Marvelous is such knowledge beyond me;
> It is impregnable; I cannot reach to it.
> Whither could I go from Your spirit,
> And whither could I run away from Your presence?
>
> (Psalm 139:1-7)

Probing Questions:

- Why does the Father need a mediator?
- Why would we need to forgive the Father?
- What does *"conciliated"* mean?

My Notes:

_____

_____

_____

_____

_____

_____

_____

_____

4

"Hosanna!"

Exult exceedingly, daughter of Zion!
Raise a joyful shout, daughter of Jerusalem!
Behold, your King shall come to you!
Righteous and bringing salvation is He.
Humble and riding on a donkey,
And on a colt, the foal of a jenny. (Zechariah 9:9)

No one who knew Yeshua wanted Him to go into Jerusalem. It was safe outside the city, but inside, the people who wanted Yeshua out of the way were plotting His assassination.

And the chief priests and the scribes sought how, laying hold of Him by guile, they should be killing Him.
(Mark 14:1b)

The religious authorities had been waiting more than three years for the opportunity to find Him guilty of something – *anything* – serious enough to bring criminal charges before the Roman authorities.

To the Pharisees, scribes, and priests, Yeshua was nothing but trouble. For Him to succeed, they would have to fail, and they weren't going to let that happen. Whole generations had been invested in establishing a comfortable religious hierarchy, where power was concentrated in the hands of a few who had grown fat and rich off the bribes and offerings of the masses. They were determined that this upstart from Nazareth was not going to bring their enterprise crashing down on their heads.

Yeshua brought me with Him to Bethany, near Jerusalem, the day before He was to enter the city. At the home of Lazarus, whom Yeshua had raised from the dead a few days earlier, He looked astonishingly relaxed, but I could feel the tension in Him. He knew He was only a few steps away from a kind of suffering that even He could not have imagined.

I stood behind Him, silent and invisible, as I witnessed what seemed to me to be the *real* "Last Supper." Martha served dinner, and Mary opened a bottle of attar – a very expensive and precious oil – and poured it on Yeshua's feet, wiping them with her hair. The rich scent of the pungent oil filled the house quickly. It was a sweet moment...until Judas piped up:

> *"Wherefore was not this attar disposed of for three hundred denarii and given to the poor?"* (John 12:5)

Yeshua looked at Judas, already knowing that he would soon give Him up to the Jewish authorities. Oh yes, Yeshua knew what Judas would do and to what end it would lead, although His expression gave nothing away. Yeshua also knew that Judas had no real interest in helping the poor, or anyone else except himself for that matter; nevertheless, Yeshua simply corrected Judas in the same way He had corrected all the disciples at one time or another.

> **"Let her be, that she should be keeping it for the day of My burial. For the poor you have always with you, yet Me you have not always."** (John 12:7-8)

Word traveled quickly in and around Jerusalem, and by morning, as Yeshua made His way toward the city, groups of people began meeting Him along the road. Their faces were as expectant as their voices were hopeful.

At first, they came in small groups, but as the distance to Jerusalem shortened, small groups grew into crowds. People seemed to pour out from villages all around Jerusalem and from inside the city. Many had collected palm branches, which they threw on the road in front of Yeshua, so that we walked with Him along a green pathway.

I felt funny walking beside Him, but that was my place if I was to learn everything He had to teach me.

Two disciples who had broken off to go into a village along the way, returned with a donkey colt. Yeshua had told them where to go and what to say when they found the donkey. They did as He said, and everything happened exactly as He told them it would.

> *Jesus dispatches two disciples, saying to them, "Go into the village facing you, and immediately you will be finding an ass, bound, and a colt with her. Loosing them, lead them to Me. And if anyone should be saying anything to you, you shall be declaring that 'The Lord has need of them.' Now straightway he will be dispatching them."* (Mathew 21:1b-3)

Yeshua mounted the animal, which had never been ridden before, but which bore Him easily and without complaint. As He approached Jerusalem, the throngs of people along the road began singing and shouting, *"Hosanna! Blessed is He Who is coming in the name of the Lord!"* and, *"The King of Israel!"* (John 12:13b).

Whenever I had heard the Scripture above quoted before, I thought that **"Hosanna"** was an expression of celebration, like *"Hooray!"* or *"Boy, are we glad to see you!"* I discovered that *Hosanna* expressed something else entirely! The word meant, *"be propitious,"*[2] or *"save us!"*[3] I was watching people not praising Yeshua so much as almost *begging* Him to establish His kingdom before their eyes. They apparently expected Him to overthrow the Roman authority like a military ruler. It was an odd image, juxtaposed with an obviously meek Man Who entered Jerusalem riding on a donkey's colt.

If anyone had bothered to look in the Scriptures, they would have known that they were witnessing the fulfillment of the prophecies concerning their Messiah, written hundreds of years before. Everything unfolded for all to see, exactly as it had been written.

I was reminded that Yeshua's entire life, from the details of His birth to the events I was witnessing, had been prophesied throughout the Old Testament. How did everyone miss the signs? How did the very people who had waited and prayed for Him to come for so long miss Him now?

I also remembered why Yeshua had invited me here: He had already lived this once; He was going through this as if it were happening all over again, *all for my benefit*. I could not afford to miss the lessons He was teaching me!

Oh Yahweh, do save us indeed!
Oh Yahweh, do prosper us indeed!
Blessed in the Name of Yahweh is He who is coming;
We bless You from the house of Yahweh.
(Psalm 118:25-26)

Probing Questions:

- Why did Yeshua seem so calm, knowing what would soon happen to Him?
- What did the disciples *really* think about what was happening?
- What does it mean to be "meek"?

My Notes:

_____

_____

_____

_____

_____

_____

_____

_____

5

Bread, Wine, and Water

> *And when the hour came, He leans back at table, and the twelve apostles with Him. And He said to them, "With yearning I yearn to be eating this Passover with you before My suffering. For I am saying to you that under no circumstances may I be eating of it till it may be fulfilled in the kingdom of God."*
>
> (Luke 22:14-16)

Yeshua seemed to be marking items off an invisible "to do" list. Each step He took was deliberate, purposeful, and fulfilled everything written about Him in the Scriptures. Yeshua was always seeing ahead; many times He knew things no one else could have, or saw things no one else could. For example, He knew where the donkey colt would be, which He rode into Jerusalem; so, it seemed to take no one by surprise when He sent Peter and John ahead to arrange a room for all of them to observe the Passover. Yeshua knew where the room was and what they should say to the owner.

Now He said to them, "Lo! at your entering into the city a man will meet with you, bearing a jar of water. Follow him into the house which he is entering. And you will be declaring to the householder of the house, saying, 'The Teacher is saying to you, "Where is My caravansary where I may be eating the passover with My disciples?"' And that man will be showing you a large upper room with places spread. There make ready." Now, coming away, they found it according as He had declared to them. (Luke 22:10-13a)

When we arrived at the house in Jerusalem, we climbed a flight of stairs to a large open room. The walls were bare and windows were cut out of three walls, one of which looked out on a courtyard behind the house. The table was set with 13 places; oddly, I had never before realized that Yeshua, together with the 12 closest disciples, made a group of 13 men.

During dinner, I watched Yeshua break a loaf of bread, and after He gave thanks to the Father, He handed John a piece, who passed the loaf around the table. Yeshua told them that the bread symbolized His body that was about to be broken for them and the whole world. As they ate, He poured some wine in a chalice and handed it to John, who passed it on to the others. He told them each to drink the wine that symbolized His blood, which was about to be spilled for them and the world. This was the first *"Lord's Supper,"* and I was watching it happen!

After dinner, Yeshua did a most remarkable thing: He took off His outer robe, tied a towel around His waist, and filled a basin with water. He looked like the lowest servant as He set the basin in front of each disciple, carefully taking their feet in His hands and washing them one by one. Peter protested at first, but when Yeshua explained the significance, Peter wanted to be totally immersed! I watched Yeshua closely as He washed Judas' feet along with the others. I thought, *"Man, how do You do that?"* The Lord looked at me as if to ask, *"You learning anything yet?"*

After everyone's feet were washed, Yeshua announced that one of them would give Him up. Yeshua didn't tell anyone who it was; instead, He made what looked to me like a very clear gesture: He said, **"He it is to whom I, dipping in the morsel, shall be handing it"** (John 13:26a). Next, He handed Judas **"the morsel,"** but no one *besides* Judas seemed to realize what was happening! Even after Yeshua sent Judas out to complete his errand, **"more quickly"** (John 13:27), the other disciples *still* didn't grasp the importance of Judas' hasty departure.

I watched the whole scene in utter amazement, and I so wanted to shake the disciples and shout, *"Hey! Wake up you guys! Doesn't anyone have a clue Who just washed your feet? Do you realize where Judas is going now and what all this means?"*

Suddenly, I felt a wave of exhaustion crash over me. Yeshua didn't need to say out loud what I heard Him say in my mind: *"Suck it up! There's more to go before either of us sleeps."*

Yeshua became intent on imparting to the disciples everything He had for them after Judas left. He was unhurried, but focused on giving them what they would need after He was no longer among them. The disciples listened intently, and Yeshua spoke to them in clear, simple language; still, the questions that Thomas and Phillip asked exposed the shrouds that covered their comprehensions. When Yeshua told them that they would all desert Him before the night was over, Peter blurted out, *"Never! Not me!"* Yeshua told him what would happen and how Peter would know that what He had said was true.

> **"Verily, I am saying to you that in this night, ere a cock crows, thrice will you be renouncing Me."** (Matthew 26:34)

Yeshua spoke to the disciples about **"the consoler...the spirit of truth"** (John 14:26, 16:13), which the Father would send after Yeshua left, to teach them and guide them **"into all the truth"** (John 16:13). Everything Yeshua told them was important, but something struck me like I'd never heard it before:

> ***Lo! The hour is coming and has come, that you should be scattered, each to his own, and you may be leaving Me alone. And I am not alone, for the Father is with Me.*** (John 16:32)

I had heard from listening to preachers, that the Father, "turned His face away" from Yeshua during His final hours. They said that the Father would not look on the world's sin, which had been heaped upon His Son; but that wasn't what Yeshua said! He said, **"I am not alone, for the Father is with Me"** (John 16:32b).

Suddenly, I realized I'm not alone *either*, for the Father is with *me too*! Even when I think I've "lost it" and nothing looks right, nothing seems to be working out, and I'm at the end of myself, **"the Father is with me."** He may be *silent*, but He is **"with me."**

Everything in me breathed an enormous sigh of relief as I grasped that Yeshua's statement applied to me as much as it did to Him. I was *never* alone; I only *thought* I was! The Father was *silent*, but not *absent*; in fact, He was *with* me – He *IS* with me (and *you*) – ALL the time!

The Lord glanced in my direction and I could hear His voice in my mind: *"You like that, huh? Well, stay sharp, 'cause this isn't over yet."*

Yeshua ended the time with His disciples by addressing the Father on their behalf in the most stirring prayer, captured in the 17th chapter of John's Gospel. As Yeshua spoke to His Father, I closed my eyes and listened to His voice. I had *read* His words dozens of times, but *hearing* Him now was a completely new and wonderful experience. Within Yeshua's prayer was the only declaration He ever made of His title, *"HaMashiach,"* in Hebrew, or *"the Messiah."*

When I heard Yeshua speak, I recognized that this **"Son of Mankind"** (Matthew 8:20), and **"Son of God"** (Luke 1:35) was heard in Heaven and His prayer was most assuredly answered by His Father. I've long known that the Father does not waste time, lives, or words, least of all His own Son's.

Whenever I read Yeshua's words in John's account, I hear the Father answering His prayer for you and me today.

> *Father, come has the hour. Glorify Thy Son, that Thy Son should be glorifying Thee, according as Thou givest Him authority over all flesh, that everything which Thou hast given to Him, He should be giving it to them, even life eonian. Now it is eonian life that they may know Thee, the only true God, and Him Whom Thou dost commission, [Yeshua HaMasiach].*
>
> *I glorify Thee on the earth, finishing the work which Thou hast given Me, that I should be doing it.*

And now glorify Thou Me, Father, with Thyself, with the glory which I had before the world is with Thee. I manifest Thy name to the men whom Thou givest Me out of the world. Thine they were, and to Me Thou givest them, and Thy word they have kept. Now they know that all, whatever Thou hast given Me, is from Thee, for the declarations which Thou hast given Me, I have given them, and they took them, and know truly that I came out from Thee, and they believe that Thou dost commission Me.

Concerning them I am asking. Not concerning the world am I asking, but concerning those whom Thou hast given Me, for they are Thine. And Mine all are Thine, and Thine Mine. And I have been glorified in them. And no longer am I in the world, and they are in the world, and I to Thee am coming. Holy Father, keep them in Thy name, in which Thou hast given them to Me, that they may be one, according as We are. When I was with them in the world, I kept those whom Thou hast given Me in Thy name, and I guard them, and not one of them perished, except the son of destruction, that the scripture may be fulfilled. Yet now to Thee am I coming, and these things am I speaking in the world that they may be having My joy filled full in themselves.

I have given them Thy word. And the world hates them, for they are not of the world, according as I am not of the world. I am not asking that Thou shouldst be taking them away out of the world, but that Thou shouldst be keeping them from the wicked. Of the world they are not, according as I am not of the world. Hallow them by Thy truth. Thy word is truth.

According as Thou dost dispatch Me into the world, I also dispatch them into the world. And for their sakes I am hallowing Myself, that they also may be hallowed by the truth. Yet not concerning these only am I asking, but also concerning those who are believing in Me through their word, that they may all be one, according as Thou, Father, art in Me, and I in Thee, that they also may be in Us, that the world should be believing that Thou dost commission Me.

And I have given them the glory which Thou has given Me, that they may be one, according as We are One, I in them and Thou in Me, that they may be perfected in one, and that the world may know that Thou dost commission Me and dost love them according as Thou dost love Me.

Father, those whom Thou hast given Me, I will that, where I am, they also may be with Me, that they may be beholding My glory which Thou has given Me, for Thou lovest Me before the disruption of the world. Just Father, the world, also, knew Thee not, yet I knew Thee. And these know that Thou dost commission Me.

And I make known to them Thy name, and I shall make it known, that the love with which Thou lovest Me may be in them, and I in them. (John 17)

Probing Questions:

- How was Yeshua able to treat Judas like everyone else? What's the lesson for us today?
- Why did the disciples seem not to grasp what was happening?

My Notes:

_____

_____

_____

_____

_____

You Think YOU Have it Tough?

6

Watch and Pray

> *And He is taking Peter and James and John aside with Himself, and He begins to be overawed and depressed. And He is saying to them, "Sorrow-stricken is My soul to death. Remain here and watch."*
>
> (Mark 14:33-34)

The night was cool as we hiked across the Kedron winter brook and up to the Mount of Olives. When we left the upper room, no one knew what was about to happen, except Yeshua and me. After a few minutes, we came to a garden called Gethsemane, where Yeshua and His disciples had been many times before. He took Peter, James, and John further into the garden and asked them to wait for Him and watch as He went off to pray. Everyone else stood at the garden entrance or found a spot to sit and wait.

Yeshua walked alone to the furthest point of the garden and fell on His knees. This is what I thought He must have wanted most for me to see, because here He was entirely human. I witnessed His agony as He begged the Father for another way – *any other way* – than the path He knew He was about to take. When He was exhausted from the effort, we went back to check on the three disciples who were supposed to be watching; instead, we found them dozing. Even though I had read the story many times that I was now witnessing, I found myself incredulous that the three men closest to Yeshua couldn't seem to keep their eyes open. *"Don't you realize what's about to happen?"* I thought. Yeshua didn't seem surprised that they were unable to wait, watch, and pray, but He did seem disappointed. I know I was. Then Yeshua spoke in a way that neither they nor I had heard before:

"Sorrow-stricken is My soul to death." (Matthew 26:38a)

Yeshua's words hit hard. Peter, James, and John were embarrassed, as well they ought to have been. They straightened up as Yeshua turned to go back into the garden, where He dropped to the ground in agony again. His struggle this time was of such force that I saw drops of blood form on His forehead and fall to the ground. While I stood by Him, an angel appeared and put his arm around Yeshua's shoulders, holding Him close. I felt sick.

Yeshua rose and went back to check on the three "watchers," who had fallen asleep again. Waking Peter with a nudge of His sandal, Yeshua said, **"Simon, are you drowsing? Are you not strong enough to watch one hour?**

Watch and pray lest you may be entering into trial. The spirit indeed is eager, yet the flesh is infirm" (Mark 14:37b-38). Yeshua turned away and went to the far end of the garden again, where He prayed a third time.

> *"Abba, Father, all is possible to Thee. Have this cup carried aside from Me. But not what I will, but what Thou!"* (Mark 14:36)

There, kneeling in the garden, Yeshua became to me fully identified with all mortal humanity. He was only a few hours away from suffering one of the most brutal, painful, and publicly humiliating deaths imaginable. Crucifixion caused death by the slow suffering of dehydration, or asphyxiation from the weight of a man's body restricting his lungs. Victims were left hanging for as long as it took them to die. Sometimes, the authorities would order a man's legs to be fractured to wipe out any remaining support. This is what Yeshua faced, and He wanted out if at all possible! Who could blame Him?

There was no alternative really, and Yeshua knew it. The Father's purpose was what He had agreed to fulfill before the world was even made, and its fulfillment was more important than Yeshua's agonizing desire to avoid the painful death that awaited Him.

Yeshua stood up, having made His decision, went to His friends, and told them that the authorities were coming. He walked obediently and deliberately right into the midst of the multitude that arrived to seize Him.

What a crowd there was! Many were there who had heard Yeshua teaching in the Temple. Why did no one arrest Him there? Now they came to Gethsemane armed with swords and clubs, as if to drag off a common criminal.

Judas stepped out from the crowd, walked up to Yeshua, and kissed Him, saying, **"Rejoice, Rabbi!"** (Matthew 26:49). It was an odd greeting, to say the least!

Only Yeshua's faith in the Father's promise not to leave Him dead enabled Him to walk through everything that followed. He looked at me and I heard His voice in my mind saying, *"Stay with Me. I'm going through this now for you, so make it count."* I just wanted it all to be over. I knew what was coming; I had read the story. Now I understood that Yeshua did *not* want to die any more than you or I do. He certainly did not *want* to suffer, except for the sovereign will of His Father Who sent Him for precisely this purpose! The recognition of all that was happening, and the divine order of it made my head spin.

> *Lo! A throng, and he who is termed Judas, one of the twelve, came before them, and he draws near [Yeshua] to kiss Him. Now [Yeshua] said to him,*

"Judas, with a kiss are you giving up the Son of Mankind?"

Now those about Him, perceiving what will be, say to Him, "Lord, shall we be smiting with a sword?" And a certain one of them smites the slave of the chief priest and amputates his right ear. Now answering, Yeshua said, "Give leave, till this-" And touching the ear, He heals him.

Now [Yeshua] said to the chief priests and officers of the sanctuary and elders who came along after Him, "As after a robber do you come out with swords and cudgels? At My being daily with you in the sanctuary, you do not stretch out your hands for Me, but this is your hour and the jurisdiction of darkness." Now apprehending Him, they led Him; they led Him into the house of the chief priest. (Luke 22:47-54)

Probing Questions:

- Why could the disciples not seem to stay awake, let alone "watch and pray"?
- Where or when are *we* falling asleep instead of watching and praying?

My Notes:

7

Silent Witness

> *Or are you supposing that I am not able to entreat My Father, and at present He will station by My side more than twelve legions of messengers? How, then, may the scriptures be fulfilled, seeing that thus it must occur?* (Matthew 26:53-54)

I walked beside Yeshua as the crowd led Him from the garden to the courtyard at the home of Annas, the former chief priest and the current chief priest's father-in-law. Many of Yeshua's captors had jeered, spat on Him, kicked and elbowed Him along the way, and it was about to become much worse. It was still night, but the large crowd showed no signs of dispersing. Annas questioned Yeshua, Who replied clearly and honestly:

> *The chief priest, then, asks Yeshua concerning His disciples and concerning His teaching. And Yeshua answered him, "I with boldness have spoken to the world. I always teach in a synagogue and in the sanctuary where all the Jews are coming together,*

and in hiding I speak nothing. Why are you asking Me? Inquire of those who have heard what I speak to them. Lo! These are aware what I said."* (John 18:19-21)

One of Annas' officers struck Yeshua across the face with the back of his hand after Yeshua answered the question. The blow was hard enough to raise a welt on Yeshua's cheekbone. Strangely enough, I felt it too.

At daybreak, Annas ordered Yeshua to be taken to his son-in-law, Caiaphas, the chief priest. By the time Yeshua arrived, the Sanhedrin had convened and witnesses were called to bring testimony of His crimes. Angry men came forward, telling lies and leveling false charges. Frustrations ran high, because no one could agree as to what they had seen Yeshua do or what they had heard Him say.

Finally, Caiaphas himself stood and confronted Yeshua, demanding that He tell the council whether He was the Messiah. Yeshua was well aware of the prophecies that were being fulfilled, and answered the chief priest directly:

"I am; and you shall be seeing the Son of Mankind sitting at the right hand of power and coming with the clouds of heaven." (Mark 14:62)

Suddenly, I heard a rooster crow. Yeshua heard it too. He turned and found Peter in the crowd, who realized at that moment that he had done exactly what Yeshua had told him earlier that he would do. Peter's face turned deathly pale and full of horror, guilt and shame. He hid his face and ran out.

> *And being turned, the Lord looks at Peter, and Peter is reminded of the declaration of the Lord, as He said to him, "Ere a cock crows today, you will be renouncing Me thrice." And coming outside, Peter laments bitterly.* (Luke 22:61-62)

Purely blind rage followed Yeshua's reply to Caiaphas. I stood beside Him, a silent, invisible witness, as the men guarding Yeshua began beating Him. They covered His head and took turns punching Him in the face and ridiculing Him.

> *And the men who are pressing Yeshua, scoffed at Him, lashing Him. And putting a covering about Him, they beat His face and inquired of Him, saying, "Prophesy! Who is it that hits You?" And many different things they said against Him, blaspheming.*
> (Luke 22:63-65)

It was still early morning when the chief priest met again with the council members, together with the scribes and elders. Once more, Caiaphas asked Yeshua, *"**If you are the Christ, tell us**"* (Luke 22:67a).

Yeshua, Who had earned a beating for answering the same question earlier, said simply, ***"If I should tell you, under no circumstances would you be believing. Yet if I should ever be asking also, under no circumstances would you be answering or releasing Me. Yet from now on the Son of Mankind shall be sitting at the right hand of the power of God"*** (Luke 22:67b-69).

Yeshua's reply infuriated the Jews even more than they were already, hardening the hearts of everyone gathered, and steeling their determination to see Him put to death. Weren't these the very people to whom Yeshua had proclaimed the Father's kingdom on Earth? Weren't they of His own race and kindred, to whom He had been sent as the Messiah, to save and prepare them for the promised kingdom of God? Now they conspired to put Him to death, and for what? For saying what the Father *gave* Him to say. They didn't know it, but they too were fulfilling the ancient prophecies.

When the Jews were finished with Yeshua, I walked with Him as they paraded Him through the streets on the way to present their case against Him before the Roman Governor, Pontius Pilate.

Who believes our report?
And the arm of Yahweh, to whom is it revealed?
He shall grow up like a young shoot before Him,
And like a root sprout out from arid earth;
He has no shapeliness nor honor that we should observe Him,
And no such appearance that we should covet Him.
He is despised and shunned of men,
A Man of pains and knowing illness,
And, as a concealing of faces from Him,
He is despised, and we judge Him of no account.

(Isaiah 53:1-3)

Probing Questions:

- What was it about Yeshua that made the Jews determined to kill Him?
- What would you have done in Peter's place?
- What purpose, if any, was served by beating Yeshua?

My Notes:

8

"Crucify!"

"Now is My soul disturbed. And what may I be saying? 'Father, save Me out of this hour'? But therefore came I into this hour. Father, glorify Thy name!" A voice, then, came out of heaven, "I glorify it also, and shall be glorifying it again!" (John 12:27-28)

The Jewish council had no authority to execute Yeshua; they would have to seek approval from the Roman government. Rome, however, would never execute someone for blasphemy, which was the charge leveled against Yeshua. Before taking Him to the Governor of Judea, the council shrewdly decided to accuse Yeshua of treason against Caesar; that was sure to get the attention of the Governor, Pontius Pilate.

This was a truly bizarre and ironic scene: The Jews were forced to seek permission from a Gentile to execute one of their own. Not only that, but they would not enter Pilate's palace, because to do so would have made them ceremonially unclean and they would not be able to celebrate Passover. At the same time, they apparently considered themselves *entirely* "clean" in bringing false charges and false testimony against Yeshua! How far from God and their own law they had fallen. Years later, the Apostle Paul would call Yeshua, *"our Passover."*

> **For our Passover also, Christ, was sacrificed for our sakes so that we may be keeping the festival, not with old leaven, nor yet with the leaven of evil and wickedness, but with unleavened sincerity and truth.**
> (1 Corinthians 5:7b-8)

Pilate went back and forth from the outer court to the audience room where Yeshua and I stood under guard. This was as far as the Jews could go without making themselves ceremonially unclean and thereby disqualified from taking part in the Passover feast. Pilate went out to hear their accusations and increasing insistence that Yeshua should be executed; then Pilate came back inside where we stood, to discover what Yeshua might say about the charges.

When Pilate asked Yeshua about the accusation that He claimed to be a king, Yeshua didn't deny it; He simply told Pilate that His kingdom was not of *this* world.

> **My kingdom is not of this world. If My kingdom were of this world, My deputies, also, would have contended, lest I should be given up to the Jews.**
> (John 18:36)

Pilate was clearly troubled and he appeared to be looking for a way out of the dilemma he confronted. He tried persuading the Jews to deal with Yeshua under their own law. The Jews, however, were adamant that Yeshua was a threat to Rome and should be executed under Roman law.

Somewhere in the Jews' accusations, Pilate spotted an opportunity to send Yeshua elsewhere. He asked Yeshua, "Are you a Galilean?"

> *[The Jews] were insistent, saying that 'He is exciting the people, teaching down the whole of Judea, beginning even from Galilee as far as here." Now Pilate, hearing "Galilee," inquires if the man is a Galilean.* (Luke 22:5-6)

Pilate left the room quickly, apparently to arrange for Yeshua to be sent to Herod Antipas, Rome's regional ruler over the Judean province that included Galilee, and who was in Jerusalem at the time. Herod was also the man who had reluctantly ordered John the Baptist's beheading, and who would later order the execution of the Apostle James. Pilate and Herod were by no means friends, and Pilate hoped to saddle Herod with Yeshua's case.

Herod knew Yeshua by reputation and seemed to be excited about meeting Him. Standing in his throne room, it looked to me as if Herod was expecting Yeshua to perform some kind of miracle for him like a court magician. He questioned Yeshua repeatedly, while Yeshua remained completely silent; He was clearly through speaking about anything to anyone. He knew He would only be wasting His breath if He were to raise any defense or protest.

Herod was obviously frustrated and he took his anger out on Yeshua, ordering an elegant robe of fine linen to be draped over Him, while Herod and his soldiers ridiculed and mocked Yeshua as they shouted, *"Hail, King of the Jews!"* (Matthew 27:29). Herod then ordered Yeshua to be sent back to Pilate, refusing to have any more to do with Him or the charges against Him.

Pilate, however, still could find no cause to put Yeshua to death and told the Jews exactly that. Pilate's wife sent him a message, urging him to release Yeshua.

> *For [Pilate] was aware that it was because of envy they give Him up. Now at his sitting on the dais, his wife dispatches to him, saying, "Let there be nothing between you and that just man, for I suffered much today in a trance because of him."* (Matthew 27:18-19)

Pilate made a final attempt to placate the Jews by ordering Yeshua to be flogged. They stripped His back, tied Him to a stake, and brought out a short whip with several leather cords coming out of a thick handle. Metal discs with sharp edges were knotted into the cords, together with bone fragments. I was horrified when I saw the whip, which was designed to tear flesh off a man's body down to the bone. The pain that this punishment inflicted, together with the loss of tissue and the bleeding it produced often killed its victim.

I wanted to shield Yeshua's body, or, better yet, to cut Him free, but I was invisible and powerless. As I looked out over the crowd, they seemed perversely delighted with themselves, though many had to look away as Yeshua's blood began to spray from His back and off the cords of the whip. How He endured this torture without losing consciousness, or dying right then was baffling!

After Yeshua's scourging, the soldiers took Him into the Praetorium where they found a scarlet robe. Wrapping it around Him, they twisted thorn branches together in the shape of a wreath and pressed it into His scalp until blood ran down His face. Then, the soldiers put a wooden staff in His hand and mockingly bowed down as they shouted, **"Rejoice! King of the Jews!"** (John 19:3). When they rose to their feet, they took turns spitting on Him and beating Him over the head with the staff.

I felt like passing out myself, or at least running away from the scene; but I had been invited to be here by the One Who was being tortured in front of my eyes. Suddenly, Isaiah's words pounded in my head:

> *Yet He was wounded because of our transgressions,*
> *And crushed because of our depravities.*
> *The discipline of our well-being was on Him,*
> *And with His welts comes healing for us.*
> *All of us, like a flock, have strayed;*
> *Each to his own way, we have turned around,*
> *Yet Yahweh Himself causes the depravity of us all to come upon Him.*
> *Hard pressed is He, and He Himself is humbled,*
> *Yet He is not opening His mouth;*
> *Like a flockling to slaughter is He fetched,*
> *And as a ewe is mute before her shearers,*
> *He is not opening His mouth.* (Isaiah 53:5-7)

The soldiers pushed Yeshua from the Praetorium back out to where Pilate sat waiting. Pilate told the crowd that he could find no cause for the death penalty, hoping that the punishment he had ordered would satisfy the Jews. He presented Yeshua to them, now bleeding freely and bruised almost beyond recognition. Instead of being satisfied, the crowd shouted, **"Crucify! Crucify Him!"** (John 19:6a).

Pilate made one last attempt to release Yeshua by invoking the custom of freeing one prisoner before the Passover festival. The two choices Pilate presented side by side were Yeshua and Bar-Abbas, a known murderer.

The Jews shouted Bar-Abbas' name over and over. Pilate held up his hand to silence the crowd. When they were quiet, he asked, **"What, then, shall I be doing with Yeshua, who is termed the Messiah?"***

The Jews answered with one voice, **"Let Him be crucified!"***

Still trying to bring about some semblance of justice, Pilate asked the crowd, **"What evil does He?"***

It was no use; the crowds kept shouting, **"Let Him be crucified!"** (*Matthew 27:22-23)

Pilate gave up Yeshua to be crucified purely at the crowd's insistence, but not before he washed his hands literally of all personal responsibility.

> **Now Pilate, perceiving that it is benefiting nothing, but rather a tumult is occurring, getting water, washes off his hands in front of the throng, saying, "Innocent am I of the blood of this just man. You will be seeing to it!"** (Matthew 27:24)

The Jews ought to have known better, but they spoke their own curse that day:

> **And, answering, the entire people said, "His blood be on us and on our children!"** (Matthew 27:25)

Yeshua was stone-faced the whole time. He looked like He had withdrawn into Himself, amassing all His remaining energy and resolve to see these events through to their inevitable conclusion. In the garden hours earlier, He had chosen to carry out the Father's will rather than His own. He determined to go through whatever it took to fulfill the Father's purpose – the purpose He had helped to shape and which He came to accomplish. He was the only One Who understood the significance of the events that continued to unfold, and He had invited me to stand with Him to see them for myself.

I thought, *"Where do You find the strength inside Yourself to endure this suffering?"* His answer came from within my own spirit: *"From the same place that you find your strength to endure whatever you think is your suffering, the place where faith lives inside you. When you feel like you don't have enough of your own, borrow Mine."*

The Scriptures that had been only words on a page before now, came flooding in from my memory. They would prove to be critical landmarks to find my way through whatever the Father had designed for my life:

> **We may be glorying also in afflictions, having perceived that affliction is producing endurance, yet endurance testedness, yet testedness expectation.**
>
> (Romans 5:3-4)

Watching the Scriptures being fulfilled before your eyes is a frightening thing to witness. There was no sense, no logic, and no reason to what the Jews did. Everything that was happening was declared through the prophets centuries earlier. The Jews who were shouting for Yeshua to be crucified had been *raised* on the Scriptures they were now fulfilling, but not one of them realized it!

> *Surely He Himself has borne our illnesses,*
> *And our pains, He was burdened with them;*
> *As for us, we accounted Him assaulted,*
> *Smitten of Elohim and humbled.*
> *From restraint and from judgment He is taken,*
> *And on His personal fate, who is meditating?*
> *For He is severed from the land of the living;*
> *Because of the transgressions of My people, He is led*
>   *to death.* (Isaiah 53:4, 8)

Probing Questions:

- Why did Pilate order Yeshua to be crucified when he knew Him to be innocent?
- Why do you think the Jewish leaders missed their own Messiah?

My Notes:

9

"Skull's Place"

Near is Yahweh to the broken of heart,
And those crushed of spirit He shall save.
Many are the evils on the righteous one,
But Yahweh shall rescue him from them all.

(Psalm 34:18-19)

Silent and sentenced, the soldiers brought Yeshua outside Pilate's palace to a yard where several enormously heavy-looking wooden poles lay mounted with crossbars. A centurion pointed to one and said, *"Pick it up; let's go."* Yeshua took a few halting steps to the cross, but He had no strength to pick it up. The centurion ordered two soldiers to put it on Yeshua's shoulders; He nearly collapsed when He tried to bear its weight. I tried to help Him, but He looked at me, silently reminding me that I was only an observer and that this was His burden to carry. I remembered His words from only a day ago:

I am not alone, for the Father is with Me. (John 16:32b)

Yeshua seemed completely alone to me. If the Father was with Him – with us here – I could not see or hear any sign of Him. Isn't that how it is, I thought, when I have been at my lowest? Truly, this is a kind of love I don't begin to comprehend; the kind that will stop at nothing short of fulfilling a purpose that must be so grand that this – even this horror – is worth its price.

Yeshua began to drag the cross along a rocky path through the streets of Jerusalem and up a hill, named, **"'Golgotha,' which is termed 'Skull's Place,'"** (Matthew 27:33). The Roman soldiers must have realized that He was never going to make it all the way by Himself, because one of them pulled a Cyrenian man named Simon out of the crowd to carry the cross up the sloping streets and all the way to the crest of the hill. Men and women along the path either wept (and I along with them) or jeered. When a woman tried giving Yeshua a drink of water, she was pushed back by the soldiers. When He stumbled and fell, the soldiers whipped and prodded Him.

Once on the hill of Golgotha, two criminals were crucified on either side of Yeshua. Though He never resisted throughout the ordeal, the soldiers held Him down, pressing His arms flat on the crossbar. One of them took a huge mallet and holding a long thick spike over Yeshua's wrist just above the end of His palm, pounded it directly through the flesh. The sound of steel tearing through skin, muscle, and vessels, was sickening. The process was repeated with Yeshua's other wrist; then, His feet were crossed one over the other, and another spike was centered over them. When the hammer came down, the spike drove through His flesh into the wood behind, miraculously passing through the joints of His feet and missing His bones.

> ***He...is guarding all His bones***
> ***So that not one of them is broken.*** (Psalm 34:20)

Yeshua was pinned, literally, and He was in tremendous pain of a kind that I cannot fathom. When the soldiers set the pole upright, Yeshua's weight shifted downward, stretching the fresh wounds in His hands and feet. All I could do was watch and weep, along with many others who stood by. There were also many who mocked Him. They had no idea that the Man they had shouted for Pilate to crucify was the Messiah for Whom all Hebrews had hoped. Shortly after the soldiers raised up His cross, I heard Yeshua say, in a weakened, pained voice, **"Father, forgive them, for they are not aware what they are doing"** (Luke 23:34a).

Yeshua's breathing became shallower and more labored in the hours that followed. At one point, He saw His mother standing with a group of women, and the disciple John also standing nearby. Yeshua gave John the care of His mother, saying to her, *"Woman, lo! Your son!"* To John, He said, *"Lo! Your mother!"* (John 19:26, 27a).

At noon, after three hours on the cross, the sky became as dark as if it were night; those who had ridiculed Him suddenly became silent. For the first time in His existence, Yeshua appeared not to be aware of His Father's presence, and He cried out loudly, *"'Eloi! Eloi! Lema sabachthani?' That is, 'My God! My God! Why didst Thou forsake Me?'"* (Matthew 27:46). Yeshua obviously felt utterly alone.

At the ninth hour (3:00 p.m.), as the Temple priest would have begun the last sacrifice of the day, I watched Yeshua die. The last words He spoke were, *"Father into Thy hands I am committing My spirit"* (Luke 23:46a), and, *"It is accomplished"* (John 19:30a). As soon as He died, the veil that separated the "holy of holies" in the Temple was torn from top to bottom, and people came out of graves that were suddenly opened! Although the religious authorities ignored these signs, many who heard of them realized that day who Yeshua was. Even a Roman centurion who was among those posted at Golgotha, said, *"Truly this was God's Son!"* (Matthew 27:54b).

A centurion came up the hill with orders to break the legs of the men who hung on crosses. The Jews had requested this of Pilate so that the bodies would not defile the Passover. The centurion gave the order and a soldier fractured the two criminals' legs, but when he came to Yeshua, he found Him already dead. The centurion, wanting to be certain, drew his sword and stabbed Yeshua's side, out of which poured blood and water.

> **And they will look to Him Whom they stabbed.**
> (Zechariah 12:10b)

Who can come close to appreciating Yeshua's agony? I asked myself, is there anything in my life – or yours – to compare with such treatment? Has anything happened to me or you that approaches that level of brutality? What, pray tell, do I think is so tough?

> **Surely He Himself has borne our illnesses,**
> **And our pains, He was burdened with them;**
> **As for us, we accounted Him assaulted,**
>   **Smitten of Elohim and humbled.** (Isaiah 53:4)

Probing Questions:

- About whom was Yeshua speaking when He asked the Father to forgive them?
- What is the significance of Yeshua's bones being left intact?
- Why and in what ways have I figuratively crucified Yeshua in my life?

My Notes:
_____
_____
_____
_____
_____
_____
_____
_____
_____

10

Another Garden

And they appoint His tomb with the wicked,
With the rich His sepulcher,
Although He had done no wrong,
And no deceit was in His mouth. (Isaiah 53:9)

A palace guard approached Pontius Pilate with an unusual question. "Sir, a man named Joseph, an Aramathean, is requesting permission to take the body of the man, Yeshua." Surprised that anyone on the cross had died so quickly, Pilate ordered a centurion to verify that Yeshua was in fact dead. When he was satisfied, the Governor gave Joseph permission to take the body.

Joseph of Aramathea believed in Yeshua, but he kept it a secret for fear of the Jews, because he was also a member of the Sanhedrin. Joseph recruited Nicodemus, another secret believer and teacher of the Law, to help him. Nicodemus brought spices of astonishing value with him to preserve Yeshua's body. The two men worked quickly to finish their preparations of spices and linen wrap, laying the body in Joseph's tomb; finally, they rolled a large stone over the opening. Mary of Magdalene and other women saw the two men place Yeshua's body in Joseph's tomb and went home to prepare more spices and perfumes for the body, according to Jewish burial customs. Meanwhile, the eleven remaining disciples waited in the room where they had eaten their last supper with the Lord only the night before.

The next morning, soldiers placed a seal on the opening of the tomb. Pilate had ordered the seal to satisfy the Jewish religious authorities who feared that Yeshua's disciples would steal the body and falsely proclaim His resurrection.

The timing of Yeshua's death was significant, because that evening began the *"Day of Preparation,"* when the Passover lamb was slaughtered for the last meal on the following day. On the first Passover, while the Israelites were preparing to leave Egypt, they put some of the lamb's blood on their doorposts as a kind of "seal" against the destroying angel who would come to kill every firstborn child in the land of Egypt. The seal was placed on Yeshua's tomb on the morning of the Day of Preparation, before the Passover meal; and the evening after would begin the Sabbath...the third day.

A flawless flockling, a year-old male, shall you come to have. From the he-lambs or from the goats shall you take it.

And it will become a charge of yours until the fourteenth day of this month. Then they will slay it, every assembly of the congregation of the sons of Israel, between the evening hours. And they will take some of the blood and put it on the two jambs and on the lintel, on the houses in which they are eating it.

Then they will eat the flesh on this night, roasted with fire, and with unleavened bread; over bitter herbs shall they eat it. Do not eat any of it underdone or cooked by being cooked in water, but rather roasted with fire, even its head along with its shanks and with its inwards. You shall not reserve any of it until the morning. And what is left of it until the morning you shall burn with fire. And thus shall you eat it, with your waist girded, your sandals on your feet and your stave in your hand. You will eat it in urgent haste. It is the passover to Yahweh.

For I will pass through the land of Egypt in this night and smite every firstborn in the land of Egypt, from human even unto beast, and on all the elohim of Egypt I shall execute judgments; I am Yahweh. Then the blood will become a sign for you on the houses where you are. When I see the blood I will pass over you. And there shall not come to be a stroke on you to cause ruin when I smite in the land of Egypt.

> **Hence this day will become for you a memorial, and you will celebrate it as a festival to Yahweh. Throughout your generations shall you celebrate it as an eonian statute.**
>
> (Exodus 12:5-14)

Probing Questions:

- What do you think was important about Yeshua's rapid death on the cross?
- Why do you think the disciples didn't believe the reports of Yeshua's resurrection?

My Notes:

_____

_____

_____

_____

_____

_____

11

The Lesson

Yet Yahweh desires to crush Him,
And He causes Him to be wounded. (Isaiah 53:10a)

I stayed near the tomb, wandering in the garden and considering what I had learned from all that I had seen and heard over the past couple of days. I wondered if the disciples found the waiting as hard as I did. Were *they* thinking about all they had learned from *their* time with Yeshua? Did anyone realize the significance of His death *or* His life? I already knew the end of the story I had been witnessing, albeit in a vision; still, I wondered if anyone was waiting as expectantly as I was for the third day.

Yeshua had brought me here to gain a better, proper perspective of what I thought was my worst experience by taking me with Him through *His* worst experience. What had I learned?

Everything boils down to identifying with Yeshua.

My success or failure in **"carrying [my] own salvation into effect,"** as the Apostle Paul wrote to the Philippians (2:12), depends on how closely and completely I identify with the Lord, as a Man and as the Son of God.

There is no greater example of faith, obedience, selflessness, sacrifice, graciousness, patience, and purposefulness, than the One Who came to show me all those qualities and, to the extent that I am willing to receive it, impart them to me.

> **[Together] with Christ have I been crucified.**
> (Galatians 2:20a)

Paul identified himself with Yeshua on the cross, and invites you and me to do likewise. Yeshua had given me an opportunity to know what identifying with Him means by walking with Him through the experience! He did *nothing* for Himself and *everything* for me. He did for me what I would never willingly do: He put Himself in the hands of people who hated Him, knowing what it would cost. He fell silent, choosing not to lift a finger or speak a word to change the course of events, even though He could have done just that.

> **"Are you supposing that I am not able to entreat My Father, and at present He will station by My side more than twelve legions of messengers?"** (Matthew 26:53)

Although Yeshua didn't show it outwardly, I certainly felt profoundly frustrated with the people around Him who barely had a clue about Who He was! That frustration was eclipsed, however, by my disappointment over the unspeakable injustice of His betrayal and rejection by those closest to Him.

As I wandered through the garden, I realized that if I have been *crucified* with the Messiah, then I *suffer* with Him. I realized the magnitude of His suffering for the first time, now that I had witnessed it. I remembered that Yeshua uttered not one word of protest or complaint, and His example forced me to recognize how far I was from His standard and from identifying with Him in my life.

Is Yeshua's standard achievable? Paul knew it was:

> **[Together] with Christ have I been crucified, yet I am living; no longer I, but living in me is Christ.**
> (Galatians 2:20a)

If the Messiah is truly living in me, I ought never to complain about anything in my life EVER! I ought never to utter a word of protest, because to do so denies that Yeshua DOES live in me!

I considered the depth of Yeshua's faith, which you and I can adopt today:

> **Now that which I am now living in flesh, I am living in faith that is of the Son of God, Who loves me, and gives Himself up for me.** (Galatians 2:20b)

The faith that I have is *OF* the Son of God. It was *His* before it could be mine and His faith fuels mine. He had it before I ever could, and He had it in the midst of the most horrible circumstances imaginable. Yeshua *alone* suffered for *all* mankind; so, His suffering and the faith He held in the face of such horror are truly beyond our comprehension.

Yeshua's faith ought to become yours and mine, if we intend to meet Him standing boldly, like Paul, knowing that we, **"contended the ideal contest...finished [our] career[s], [and]...kept the faith"** (2 Timothy 4:7).

I thought I knew about faith, but I had to admit that I did not truly KNOW it within myself like Yeshua did.

> **Now faith is an assumption of what is being expected, a conviction concerning matters which are not being observed.** (Hebrews 11:1)

Yeshua *assumed* – He regarded without questioning – the *expectation* of resurrection; He had a conviction of something He had not yet observed. Like His "father" Abraham, Yeshua *obeyed, sojourned,* and *waited*:

> **By faith Abraham, being called, OBEYS, coming out into the place which he was about to obtain to enjoy as an allotment, and came out, not versed in where he is coming. By faith he SOJOURNS in the land of**

promise as in an alien land. ... For he WAITED for the city having foundations, whose Artificer and Architect is God. (Hebrews 11:8-10, emphasis mine)

Suddenly, I felt ashamed for whining and complaining to the Father about the circumstances that brought about this visitation from the Lord. What was it about my life that I thought was so tough? Who was I kidding?

For take into account the One Who has endured such contradiction by sinners while among them, lest you should be faltering, fainting in your souls. Not as yet unto blood did you repulse, when contending against sin. (Hebrews 12:3-4)

Yeshua's disciples, even though they practically lived with Him for three and a half years, still did not have *His* revelation and therefore, they did not have *His* identity. They had their *own* identities and the revelation that Yeshua imparted to them had to filter *through* their identities until they were able – IF they were able – to give up their rights to themselves for Him.

It seemed to me, having witnessed Yeshua's attitude and actions, that to the degree I succeed in surrendering my life, just like Yeshua surrendered His to the Father's will and not His own, I can know Him, not only, as Paul says, in **"the fellowship of His sufferings,"** but also in **"the**

power of His resurrection" (Philippians 3:10). Oh, how I felt ready for the life of resurrection!

Yeshua's words came back to me as if I were hearing them for the first time. Now I knew what He meant:

> ***If anyone is wanting to come after Me, let him renounce himself and pick up his cross and follow Me. For whosoever may be wanting to save his soul shall be destroying it. Yet whoever should be destroying his soul on My account shall be finding it.*** (Matthew 16:24-25)

Yeshua's disciples found it difficult to grasp His words and the principles He taught them, even though they were with Him daily when He was alive. I now understood why I had found it hard to make sense of His words, having never laid eyes on Him in the flesh. This was a lame excuse, however, for Yeshua Himself said to another Thomas, ***"Happy are those who are not perceiving and believe"*** (John 20:29b).

I also had an advantage over the disciples because ***"the consoler"*** had been poured out on me; the Spirit of Holiness, which the Father sent in Yeshua's name (John 14:26). Paul called it, ***"an earnest of the enjoyment of our allotment"*** (Ephesians 1:14), which Yeshua said, ***"will be guiding you into all the truth"*** (John 16:13).

I had only excuses, but no reasons, for living to myself as if I owned my life and as if I had not been bought with the price of Yeshua's blood. How could I refuse to be identified with Him fully and continue living to myself, while giving only lip service to Him, if any at all? Such a foolish choice would be the epitome of what the Apostle Paul called, *"[receiving]* **the grace of God for naught"** (2 Corinthians 6:1).

The Messiah died for *you and me,* not for *Himself!* He believed that the Father would raise Him and exalt Him. Paul came along and said that the Father would do the same for you and me! How could we, knowing what we do now and having seen what we have, not count ourselves to have died with Him so that He might live in and through us, and so that we would be counted among His brethren?

There can be no resurrection without dying first; not for Yeshua and not for us either. If we are conformed to His *death*, we will be conformed also to His *life*, which will no longer be *subject* to death.

> **We, who died to sin, how shall we still be living in it? Or are you ignorant that whoever are baptized into Christ Yeshua, are baptized into His death?**
>
> (Romans 6:2b-3)

At **"the Dais of Christ"** (2 Corinthians 5:10), there is no judge, as in a courtroom where punishments are meted out; but a judge as at a reviewing stand in an athletic contest, where contestants receive awards. The criteria for your award and mine have nothing to do with the number of souls reached or good works done, but the degree to which the Scriptures were fulfilled in my life and yours, and how closely we were identified with the Lord in His death. If you and I are successful, we will have expressed the Lord in and through our lives, because our natures became His.

> **In that day you shall know that I am in My Father, and you in Me, and I in you.** (John 14:20)

Yeshua told the disciples that following Him would not be easy; He only said it would be worth the effort:

> **Enter through the CRAMPED GATE, for broad is the gate and spacious is the way which is leading away into destruction, and many are those entering through it** *[this gate is so big, any fool can find it, and most do!]*. **Yet what a CRAMPED GATE and NARROWED WAY is the one LEADING AWAY INTO LIFE, and few are those who are finding it.**
> (Matthew 7:13-14, addition and emphasis mine)

Believing, having faith, trusting the Father, dying to ourselves and living to the Messiah, are decisions you and

I make. Even when the choices run counter to our own wills, we know One Who decided to die to His own will, to believe and trust the Father, despite knowing the horror that awaited Him.

> **My Father, if it is possible, let this cup pass by from Me. However, not as I will, but as Thou!** (Matthew 26:39)

"Not as I will, but Thou!" That is the essence of faith, of trusting the Father, and deciding to do nothing of myself or for myself. What you and I learn from Yeshua is all about us, paradoxically, because everything about Him was also about us and for us, and not about Himself.

In the garden, standing outside Yeshua's tomb, I found myself facing these questions – perhaps you are facing them too:

- How much do I love Him? Enough to deny myself, pick up my cross and follow Him, no matter where it leads or what it costs?
- Do I love Him enough to know the fellowship of His sufferings before I will know the power of His resurrection?
- Do I love the Father and His Son enough for it to be said of me when I meet Him face to face:

> **[Together] with Christ have I been crucified, yet I am living; no longer I, but living in me is Christ.**

(Galatians 2:20a)

Faithful is the saying: "For if we died together, we shall be living together also; if we are enduring, we shall be reigning together also; if we are disowning, He also will be disowning us; if we are disbelieving, He is remaining faithful – He cannot disown Himself."

(2 Timothy 2:11-13)

Probing Questions:

- What does identifying with Yeshua mean to you?
- What does denying yourself look like to you?

My Notes:

_____

_____

_____

_____

12

ARISE!

**For You shall not forsake my soul in the unseen;
You shall not allow Your benign [faithful, holy[4]] one
to see corruption.** (Psalm 16:10)

Human arrogance fails to recognize that the Father does not share our limitations. In addition to the seal over the entrance to Yeshua's tomb, the Romans posted guards to make sure that no one got in. The religious and Roman authorities were prepared to prevent anyone from entering the tomb, but they were completely unprepared for Yeshua to exit the tomb! Neither the Romans nor the Jews who had insisted on these security measures, bothered to consider that Yeshua was the Messiah written about in the Scriptures, and therefore, the Father would raise Him from the dead no matter what they did.

The morning began quietly enough, and the guards at the tomb stood at ease. They must have wondered what all the fuss was about.

Suddenly, the Earth began shaking violently and an angel appeared over the tomb's entrance. He rolled away the stone and sat on it, while the fear-stricken guards shook as violently as the Earth and fell to the ground as dead men.

No one but me saw Yeshua leave the tomb early that morning. He looked radiant, relaxed, and rested, although His body bore the evidence of the scourge and the nails. He carefully folded the cloth that had covered His face and set it to the side near where His head had lain. It was a custom for a dinner guest to fold his napkin after a meal to signify that he would return. Yeshua was leaving a sign and a subtle promise that He would come to Earth again.

Yeshua looked at me and said, *"Well, have you seen enough?"* I assured Him that I had, and I thanked Him for taking me all the way through His experience to see Him rise out from among the dead. Yeshua said, *"The Father's story never ends in death but in life. As it is in My story, so it is in yours. Your faith – the assumption of your expectation and your conviction of what you cannot observe – makes life appear in your spirit today, out of what you once perceived as death. It's all about identifying with Me in My death, so that you may also identify with Me in My life!"*

When Yeshua had finished speaking, we appeared instantly in the paneled boardroom where we had begun. In the scriptural accounts, Yeshua went on to show Himself to the disciples and others, demonstrating His resurrection life with signs and miracles for 40 days, before ascending into Heaven and taking His seat at the Father's right hand.

The Father was still seated at the head of the table and I could feel Him watching me, knowingly. Yeshua and I took our seats and, as Yeshua leaned forward, with His palms outstretched on the table, He said, *"Now, what was it you were complaining about?"*

"Nothing at all, Lord," I said. *"Please forgive me. I have nothing whatsoever to complain about, and much more for which to be thankful to You and to our Father."*

Yeshua looked at me intently and said, *"No further or higher price can be exacted than My life, for whatever suffering you may endure. By your simple faith in Me, the Father reckons you as righteous; your faith in Me frees Him to lavish His grace – His joyful favor – upon you, along with saving your soul out of death and into eonian life; as My Apostle Paul wrote,* **'and this is not out of you; it is God's approach present'**" (Ephesians 2:8).

A fresh recognition of the Father's love washed over me. Yeshua made sure I appreciated the impact fully:

Did you get that, Brother? You can't earn the Father's joyful favor; it's His offering – His "approach present" – to you! That's right, the Father approaches you with His offering!

In all of Scripture, *people* brought *"approach presents"* to God; sacrifices for atonement and forgiveness. His people did not have His grace; their only hope of righteousness was strict adherence to the Law. Sacrifices – and there were lots of them – were *required* to make up for their inability to live perfectly.

Yeshua continued:

My example is the only one you have of a life lived wholly to the Father and for His purpose...all the way to death. You now know that my suffering before and on the cross was greater than any you could possibly undergo. My own experience is the only evidence on the Father's side – and it is sufficient – of how great His purpose is, how important you are to its fulfillment, how precious you are, and how worth the price I paid for you.

What you cannot know is what it was like for me to empty myself of the Glory I had before the beginning of all things: immortal, sitting next to the Father, having a hand in creating everything, and in on His whole plan from start to finish. I agreed to become completely human and die willingly as a sacrifice for all the sins committed by everyone for all time. You – and all mankind – would then have an opportunity to believe and trust the Father for yourself, get over the sentence of death and make friends with the One Who imposed it!

I agreed to lay down my life, knowing that when it looked to everyone like my mission had failed, and even the Father was silent toward me, I would have His word, as you do now, in the face of evidence that could discourage your trust. I knew that the experience would hurt (because humans feel hurt) and that it would result in my death. My faith was that the Father would not leave me dead but would raise me up and restore my glory.

I agreed to be crucified to accomplish two goals: First, to be the sacrifice that saves everyone from the sin that separated mankind from God; that separation no longer exists, all debts are settled, all sins are forgiven, and offenses are no longer reckoned. When I died, God "conciliated" the world to Himself – He ended all cause for estrangement and enmity toward Him, and brought the whole world into a state of harmony with Himself (although most of the world still doesn't know it).

The second goal was to establish the Father's credibility, vindicate His character and validate His purpose. I could lay down my life, but only He could save it by raising me from the grave. The Father fulfilled His promise to me and He extends it to you by your faith in me.

The Father now approaches you, and all who choose to believe in me and share my faith, with His offering of salvation out of death into life beyond its reach. You were crucified with me and you will surely live with me. Your acceptance of the Father's approach present – your conciliation to Him for My sake – ends your estrangement from Him, brings you into harmony with Him, and makes my sacrifice count.

> So that, if anyone is in Christ, there is a new creation: the primitive passed by. Lo! There has come new!
>
> Yet all is of God, Who conciliates us to Himself through Christ, and is giving us the dispensation of the conciliation, how that God was in Christ,

conciliating the world to Himself, not reckoning their offenses to them, and placing in us the word of the conciliation.

For Christ, then, are we ambassadors, as of God entreating through us. We are beseeching for Christ's sake, "Be conciliated to God!" For the One not knowing sin, He makes to be a sin offering for our sakes that we may be becoming God's righteousness in Him. (2 Corinthians 5:17-21)

Today, my role is that of mediator between you and the Father. When you cried out to Him, I came to help you make peace with Him. He is already at peace with you and all mankind by virtue of my sacrifice. It remains only for you to accept His open hand of friendship through the conciliation, and come into harmony with Him.

You thought you had it tough, but this fresh perspective has transformed your misery into victory! The insight you gained by walking by my side changed the view of your own journey, didn't it? From now on, you'll know that I am inside you. You invited me there and everything you experience, I do too. Your life looks different now, doesn't it?

You will recall our journey together often and it will sustain you through the years to come. Remember, I am with you always.

I looked in the Father's direction and said, "*Father, I apologize for my whining and complaining. I repent; I choose today to change my mind, from seeing my life through the limits of human vision, to seeing my situations, circumstances, and relationships through Your eyes, to the best of my ability. Bless You both for helping me gain Your perspective that is not limited to death, but issues into life that is far better and far beyond dying. Thank you. I'm ready now.*"

Then, the Father spoke for the first time:

Before the world was, I designated for you the place of a son, in accord with the delight of My will. When you believe in the sacrifice that Yeshua provided and the saving of your soul into the life that His resurrection promises, you need not hold your own life's troubles or even your own dying against Me; rather, you can forgive Me, be conciliated to Me, and we can be Friends.

You share in Yeshua's reward of life in glory with Me as surely as you share in His death. I pour out My grace over you freely now, and I will raise you also from the dead in a body like Yeshua's, and seat you together with Him among the celestials.

The Father and Yeshua both smiled as the vision ended. Opening my eyes, I sat up in bed to look out into the night sky. Almost no time had passed since the vision began and I eventually drifted off into a sound sleep. When I awoke, I began my day with renewed strength, joy, purpose, and a certainty that I had never had before. Even more importantly, a sense of profound peace settled in my spirit, soul and body. I knew that no matter what life looked like on any particular day, I could draw on my experience with Yeshua and remember that no challenge in this life would ever approach the magnitude of His suffering. I also knew that I could walk daily in the light of His life and allow it to penetrate through all of mine.

Yeshua bore the weight of *every* sin and offense, no matter what it was, who committed it or when. He was *made* the sacrifice for the forgiveness of *all* sin **"once for all time"** (Hebrews 7:27, 9:12, 10:10).

Yeshua showed me, simply by His example, that focusing on my own suffering misses the celebration found in the power of His life in me! It is one thing to identify myself with His death; it is quite another to identify myself with His life.

> *Yet when the kindness and fondness for humanity of our Saviour, God, made its advent, not for works which are wrought in righteousness which we do, but according to His mercy, He saves us, through the bath*

of renascence* and renewal of holy spirit, which He pours out on us richly through Jesus Christ, our Saviour, that, being justified in that One's grace, we may be becoming enjoyers, in expectation, of the allotment of life eonian. (Titus 3:4-7)

*"**Renascence**": "*Moral renovation, regeneration, the production of a new life consecrated to God, a radical change of mind for the better. Commonly: the restoration of a thing to its pristine state, its renovation, as the renewal or restoration of life after death.*"⁵

"**It is accomplished.**" (John 19:30a)

Probing Questions:

- What does "repent" mean?
- What is the difference between repentance and apologizing?
- What areas of your life could benefit from repentance?

My Notes:

88 ~ You Think YOU Have it Tough?

13

No More Whining!

> *For I am reckoning that the sufferings of the current era do not deserve the glory about to be revealed for us.* (Romans 8:18)

The closer you and I identify with Yeshua's *humanity*, the more we recognize our *divinity*. As the **"Son of Mankind"** (Matthew 8:20), Yeshua was as human as you and I; He did not want to die any more than we do, knowing that death is an end to all awareness; then add to that His knowledge of the treatment He would endure and the kind of death He would suffer. Can't we relate to Him completely in His experience? As the **"Son of God"** (Luke 1:35), Yeshua also showed us that we are as *divine* as He is because of what He accomplished by His death and what the Father accomplished through His resurrection.

When you and I fully grasp the power of resurrection from death into life, our own dying process becomes almost inconsequential. Neither Yeshua's nor our present mortality can be compared to the shining promise of immortality that awaits us upon His return as, **"Firstborn among many brethren"** (Romans 8:29).

What is there to whine about? Whenever you and I think we have it tough, chances are, our conditions pale in comparison to Yeshua's, and He did it *for us*.

We may not like everything we see in our lives or in the world around us, and there may be times when we feel pain. Suffering is worthwhile, however, when it serves the purpose for which we were created and leads to its fulfillment. This understanding doesn't *stop* suffering, but it helps keep us from being overwhelmed by it.

When we are truly in tune with the Father, as Yeshua was, we may even find within us a well of gratitude for the Father's purpose being accomplished in and through our lives. We discover the willingness and capacity to pay whatever price His purpose in our lives costs us, knowing it will never match Yeshua's. We will find peace in trusting the Father, into Whose hands Yeshua committed His life, and into Whose hands we can confidently commit ours.

Events, situations, circumstances, and relationships may look far less than perfect; yet, in the midst of all that we may wish were different, our Father lavishes His grace on us. He does not play games, and He does not waste time, lives, or words. His love and Yeshua's surrounds, infuses, strengthens, and comforts us, because we *believe* the Father ... because we *trust* Him.

Today we have a *choice* to love the Father even in the midst of the obvious evil in the world and the immediate challenges in our lives. The record of the Scriptures is our only evidence that the Father is trustworthy; therefore, our faith is no small thing when we exercise it. The choice we make in favor of the Father's righteousness, our agreement with His purpose, and all that the operating of His purpose requires in our lives and in the world, is a monumental decision!

We share Yeshua's faith when we believe and trust the Father. When we identify with Yeshua in His death, we identify with Him in His life now. Through faith, we become the Father's demonstration on the Earth of His wisdom, the vindication of His character, and the validation of His purpose to mankind, but even more importantly, to the celestial sovereignties and authorities.

> *Yet God, being rich in mercy, because of His vast love with which He loves us (we also being dead to the offenses and the lusts), vivifies us together in Christ (in grace are you saved!) and rouses us together and seats us together among the celestials, in Christ Jesus, that, in the oncoming eons, He should be displaying the transcendent riches of His grace in His kindness to us in Christ Jesus.* (Ephesians 2:4-7)

Our faith seats us among the celestials, where we will both witness and take part in the fulfillment of the Father's *"purpose of the eons."*

> *...in accord with the purpose of the eons, which He makes in Christ Jesus, our Lord; in Whom we have boldness and access with confidence, through His faith.* (Ephesians 3:11-12)

In the name of the One Who died to make it possible, I invite you to share, *"Jesus Christ's faith"* (Galatians 3:22 and Romans 3:22), forgiving God for your own pain and suffering, holding on to His promise of life with the Lord throughout the eons. Will you make Yeshua's sacrifice count fully by choosing faith over fear, conciliation over contempt, trust over suspicion, and love over enmity?

In the most unlikely time and place, where death, depravity, and distractions of every surround us, the Father is inviting you to share Yeshua's *glory*! Looking beyond whatever suffering you may experience, the Father is drawing near with His offering of salvation into life. When you say, *"Yes,"* heaven and earth celebrate together, and the Father's *"multifarious wisdom [is] made known to the sovereignties, and authorities among the celestials"* (Ephesians 3:10).

Nothing in your life has escaped the Father's attention. It's all purposed and its price has already been paid; so be thankful, son or daughter of God! Believe in Yeshua the Messiah, and thereby trust the Father. He is faithful and good, and His word is true. He raised Yeshua from the dead and made Him alive again, and He will do the same for you!

> **This corruptible must put on incorruption, and this mortal put on immortality.** (1 Corinthians 15:53)

> **Blessed be the God and Father of our Lord Jesus Christ, Who blesses us with every spiritual blessing among the celestials, in Christ, according as He chooses us in Him before the disruption of the world, we to be holy and flawless in His sight, in love designating us beforehand for the place of a son for Him through the Messiah Yeshua; in accord with the delight of His will, for the laud of the glory of His grace, which graces us in the Beloved: in Whom we are having the deliverance through His blood, the forgiveness of offenses in accord with the riches of His grace, which He lavishes on us; in all wisdom and prudence making known to us the secret of His will (in accord with His delight, which He purposed in Him) to have an administration of the complement of the eras, to head up all in Christ – both that in the heavens and that on the earth – in Him in Whom our lot was cast also, being designated beforehand according to the purpose of the One Who is operating all in accord with**

the counsel of His will, that we should be for the laud of His glory, who are pre-expectant in the Christ.
(Ephesians 1:3-12)

Probing Questions:

- What part of Yeshua's humanity can you identify with most?
- What areas of your own humanity need the most work to look like Yeshua?
- What part of Yeshua's *divinity* can you identify with most?

My Notes:

_____

_____

_____

_____

_____

No More Whining!

14

Believe It or Not

Holy Father...Hallow them by Thy truth. Thy word is truth. (John 17:11b, 17)

The Father's truth is absolute and what we *think* or *believe* has no effect on it. Likewise, the Scriptures are either true or they aren't; the events recorded happened or they didn't. Either the authors recorded history and prophecy by inspiration from the Father, or they made it all up.

A popular notion today suggests that truth is relative and changeable from person to person and situation to situation. It is not unusual to hear someone say something like, *"Everyone has their own truth. What's true for me may not be true for you."* This kind of empty platitude fosters doubt and indecisiveness about *whether* God is, let alone *Who* He is. To me, the spirit behind modern relativism, humanism, and situational ethics, is the same one that deceived Eve in the garden with a simple question, **"Did God really say?"** (Genesis 3:1b).

In his book, *God's Eonian Purpose*,[6] Adlai Loudy made a compelling case for the veracity of the Scriptures as the Father's inspired word. Loudy used facts and logic to contrast the Scriptures from all other writings on which men and women base their faith, build the foundation for their lives, and through which they learn the truth about the Father and His purpose. Of all the facts that Mr. Loudy examined, I found these to be the most striking:

> *Twenty-five specific predictions* were made by the Hebrew prophets, bearing on the "betrayal," "death," and "burial" of Christ. These were uttered by *different* prophets during a period of 500 years, from 1000 B.C. to 500 B.C., yet they were *all fulfilled in one twenty-four hour period by one person*—the Christ of Whom they spoke.
>
> Apply the law of "compound probabilities" to this and the chance becomes decreased to 1 in 33,554,432 that the twenty-five predictions would be fulfilled! Should one prophet make several predictions as to some one event, he might by collusion with others bring it to pass. But when a number of prophets, distributed over five centuries of time, give detailed and specific predictions as to some particular event, the charge of collusion cannot be sustained. The only way to satisfactorily account for these marvelous facts is to admit that the writers were

inspired, and the message they have given us is God's word – His revelation to mankind. (Page 27)

The truthfulness, accuracy, and usefulness of the Scriptures won't be in question when Yeshua is here on the Earth again; the hard evidence of His literal presence will replace faith. Today, faith is more valuable to the Father and carries a higher reward, precisely because it is *without* evidence.

The historical account supporting the vision in this story can be found in the four gospel accounts. Reading them now may be a new experience, having gained a fresh perspective from sharing the encounter with Yeshua and the lessons learned from it. *The Daily Bible in Chronological Order*, by F. LaGard Smith, is an excellent way to combine all four Gospels into one cohesive account.

The areas of Scripture in which the events of this book took place may be found in the following accounts:
- Matthew 26-28
- Mark 14-16
- Luke 22-24
- John 12-21

Actual quotations from the Scriptures were taken from the *Concordant Literal Versions* of the Old and New Testaments. First published in 1926, the *Concordant*

Versions are uniquely accurate translations of ancient Hebrew and Greek manuscripts.

In the early twentieth century, a German scholar, A.E. Knoch, developed a method to find the nearest modern equivalent for every Hebrew or Greek word and use it consistently throughout the translating process. According to explanatory notes in the *Concordant Literal Versions*, the word *concordant*, means, *"agreeing, correspondent, harmonious, consonant"* (Webster's Third International Dictionary). The concordant method minimizes human, religious or doctrinal bias, as the translator must be consistent in his or her renderings, while always seeking to be faithful to the Hebrew and Greek texts themselves.

At some point, you and I choose what or whom we will believe, and also what or whom we will serve. I've found that trusting, believing, or serving anything or anyone other than the Father does not work well. The more I've come to know Him, the more I've come to love Him.

What about you? What or Whom will you choose to believe, trust, and serve?

> **Choose for yourselves today whom you shall serve, whether those elohim that your fathers had served when they dwelt across the Stream, or whether the elohim of the Amorite in whose land you are dwelling; yet I and my house, we shall serve Yahweh.** (Joshua 24:15)

Probing Questions:

- How can we determine what or whom we are serving today?
- What might it cost you to believe and serve the Father?

My Notes:
_____
_____
_____
_____
_____
_____
_____
_____

You Think YOU Have it Tough?

15

Is There More?

Whatever is true, whatever is grave, whatever is just, whatever is pure, whatever is agreeable, whatever is renowned – if there is any virtue, and if any applause, be taking these into account.

(Philippians 4:8)

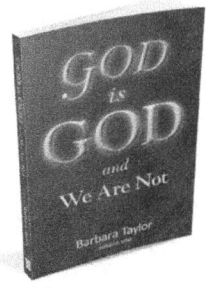

God is God And We Are Not is your ticket straight into the Father's heart.

Learn how to live in the *"Realm of the Miraculous"* today, in Barbara Brown's true story of divine healing and living by faith every day. Barbara brings *"Heaven's View"* into the details of modern life and makes faith practical today. You'll discover that the Father is *more* real and present than you ever imagined!

Available in paperback with free shipping at
BarbaraBrown.com
Also available on Amazon in paperback and KINDLE versions

Discover the One Who said,
"**Let there be YOU!**"

- Dig God out from under 2,000 years of religious tradition!
- Pull away the mystery and reveal an approachable Father you've always hoped to find!
- Discover simple answers you've always wanted to important questions you've always had!
- See God from a fresh perspective you never knew was possible

"When you seek me, you will find Me,
provided you seek for Me wholeheartedly."
(Jeremiah 29:13 Complete Jewish Bible)

Available in paperback with free shipping at
BarbaraBrown.com
Also available on Amazon in paperback and KINDLE versions

www.**WholeLifeWholeHealth**.com

"Light Up the Scriptures"

Welcome to an honest exploration of God's inspired word.

We aren't theologians, just earnest students with a passion for the Father's word with His heart, and a fresh perspective based on *"correctly cutting the word of [the] truth"* (2 Timothy 2:15).

The live teleconference happened every Tuesday night for 42 months. Every study was recorded and is available today as MP3 recordings at **LightUpTheScriptures.com**.

Blessings and joy in the journey,

Dr. Tom Taylor and *Barbara Brown, MSE*

"Morning Magicals"

Your day can start with what Barbara Brown calls the "**Morning Magicals**" (Magical here is short for "Magical Moment").

Join her in the presence of God and one another to set the tone for the day. The morning readings of the "*Scripture of the Day*" from Bible Gateway often provides a springboard for a conversation that follows.

It's all completely informal and spontaneous, and lots of folks all over the world enjoy listening to the recordings every day.

What about you?

Learn more at *www.MorningMagicals.com*.

Blessings and joy in the journey,

Barbara Brown, MSE

Whole Life Whole Health
Divine Health is Your Original Design

A life-changing wellness resource and community for true health seekers to create a life of freedom, purpose and joy, by delivering an easy to follow roadmap that supports your body, mind and spirit with direction, education and resources that you can easily master for life..

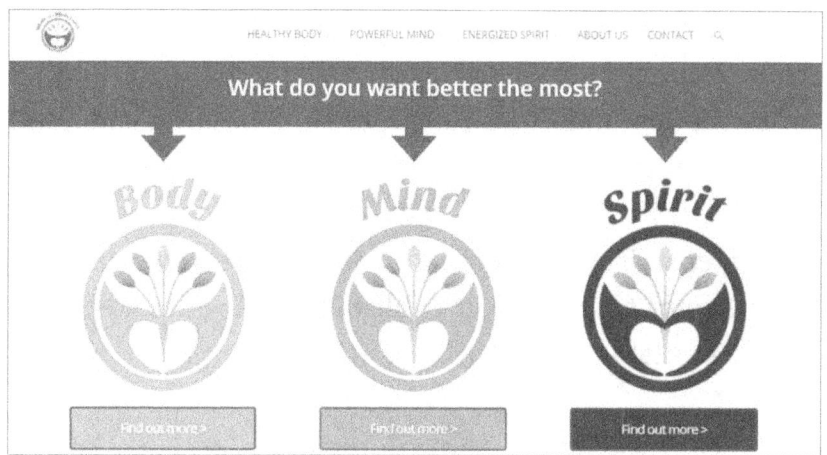

www.**WholeLifeWholeHealth**.com

References

1. ***Concordant Literal New Testament with Keyword Concordance***, Concordant Publishing Concern, P.O. Box 449, Almont, MI 48003-0449, www.concordant.org

2. ***Concordant Greek Text***, Concordant Publishing Concern

3. ***God's Eonian Purpose***, Adlai Loudy, Concordant Publishing Concern (also available online)

4. ***The Pentateuch and Haftorahs***, Hebrew Text, English Translation and Commentary, edited by Dr. J. H. Hertz, Soncino Press

5. ***Thayer's Greek-English Lexicon of the New Testament***, Zondervan Publishing, Grand Rapids, MI. Also available online at BlueLetterBible.org

6. ***The Daily Bible in Chronological Order***, F. LaGard Smith, Harvest House Publishers, Eugene, Oregon

Online Sources

- www.concordant.org
- www.biblegateway.com
- www.blueletterbible.org
- www.wikipedia.org – Greek alphabet
- www.scripture4all.org –
    Hebrew and Greek interlinear texts
- www.biblos.com – online "Bible Suite"
- www.merriam-webster.com

About the Author

Dr. Tom Taylor takes over 40 years of passion for the scriptures, translated from their original languages, and blows the lid off traditional beliefs about who God really is, who we are to Him, what His purpose is, why we're really here, and why it's important to know! He was the host of the weekly study via teleconference, "**Light Up the Scriptures**," and the developer of the blog site, "**ScriptureDoc.com**."

Dr. Taylor is recognized as an expert in bio-energetics and practical nutrition, focusing on solutions that help restore, sustain, and improve health and well-being 100% of the time. "*Anything less,*" he says, "*means you are someone's science experiment.*" He has trained health care practitioners from around the world in his specialties, written dozens of professional articles, and led numerous seminars for the public around the U.S.

Go to **www.WholeLifeWholeHealth.com** to learn more about Dr. Taylor.

Our Other Books and E-Books

(Click any photo below to learn more)

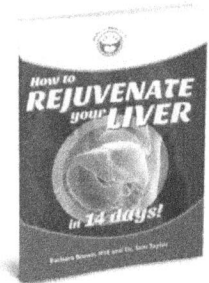

Divine Health Is Your Original Design

www.WholeLifeWholeHealth.com

Endnotes

---

[1] Thayer's online Lexicon at BlueLetterBible.org.
[2] ibid
[3] Concordant Literal New Testament Keyword Concordance (CLNT-KC), page 148
[4] Thayer's online Lexicon at BlueLetterBible.org.
[5] ibid
[6] © 1929, Concordant Publishing Concern, Almont, MI, concordant.org

My Notes:

_____

_____

_____

_____

_____

_____

My Notes:

My Notes:

My Notes:

My Notes:

My Notes:

My Notes:

My Notes:

My Notes:

My Notes:

My Notes:

My Notes:
___

www.ingramcontent.com/pod-product-compliance
Lightning Source LLC
LaVergne TN
LVHW020934090426
835512LV00020B/3350